MICKEY'S PRACTICE WORKBOOKS

MULTIPLICATION

By Margery Altman
Illustrated by Walt Disney Productions

ISBN: 0-448-16125-7
Copyright © MCMLXXVIII Walt Disney Productions.
World Wide Rights Reserved.
Printed in the United States of America
Published simultaneously in Canada

Published by WONDER BOOKS
A Division of Grosset & Dunlap
A Filmways Company
Publishers · New York

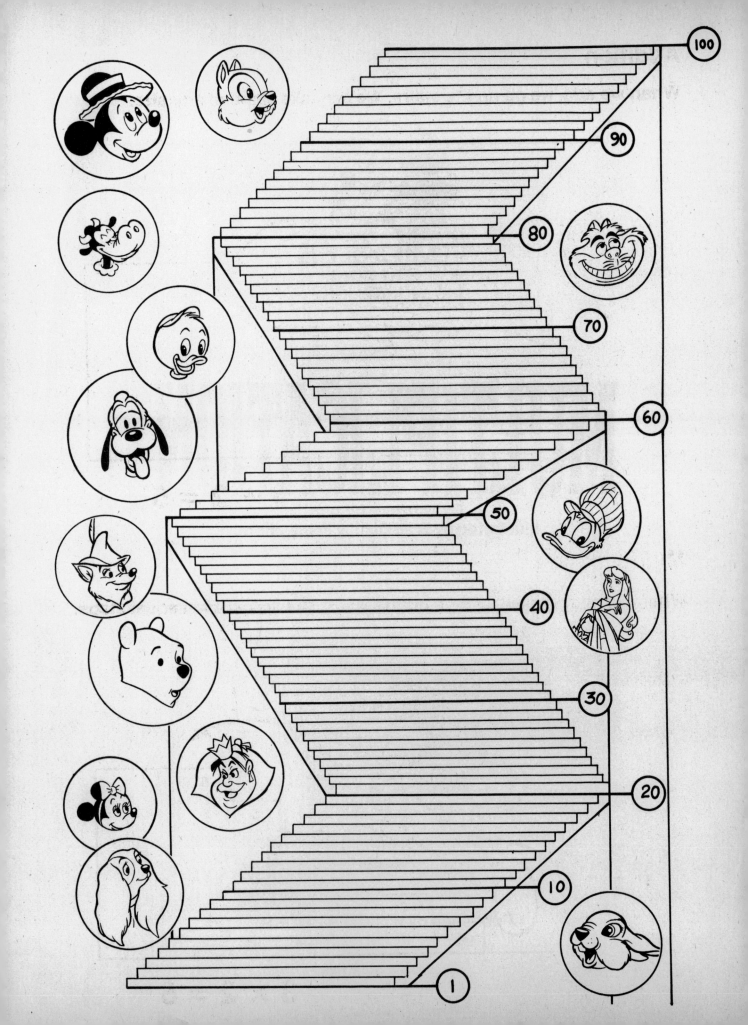

Addition

When we add, we go up the stairs. We can take steps of any size.

$$3 + 2 = 5$$

Multiplication

When we multiply, we also go up the stairs. But we go up in equal steps.

$$3 \times 2 = 6$$

 the right word. Write the numbers.

Add   Multiply

$$\boxed{} \times \boxed{} = 6$$

Add   Multiply

$$\boxed{} \times \boxed{} = 8$$

Add   Multiply

$$\boxed{} + \boxed{} = 7$$

(Circle) the right word. Write the numbers.

Add   Multiply

$$\boxed{} \times \boxed{} = 10$$

Add   Multiply

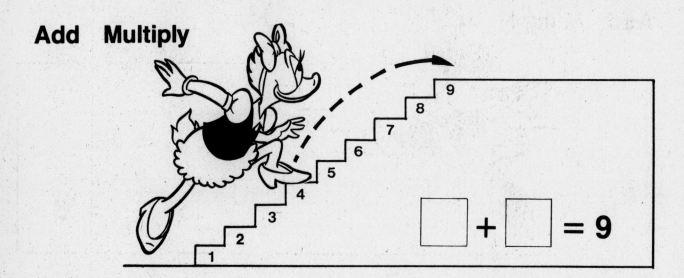

$$\boxed{} + \boxed{} = 9$$

Add   Multiply

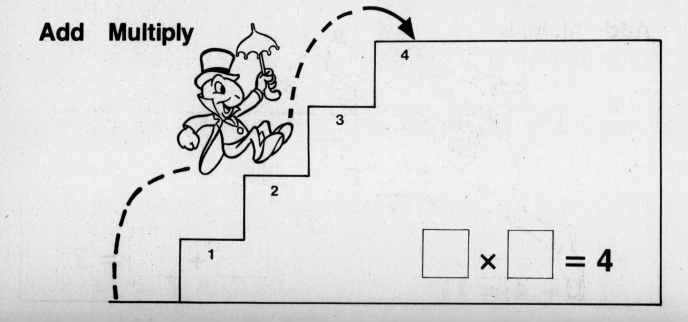

$$\boxed{} \times \boxed{} = 4$$

Mark the steps.

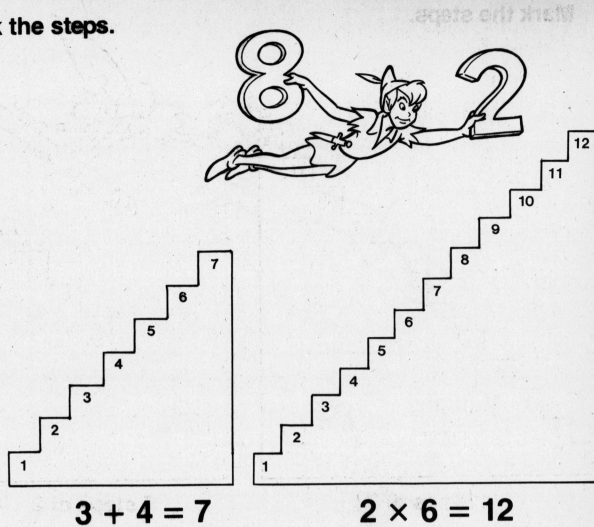

$$3 + 4 = 7$$

$$2 \times 6 = 12$$

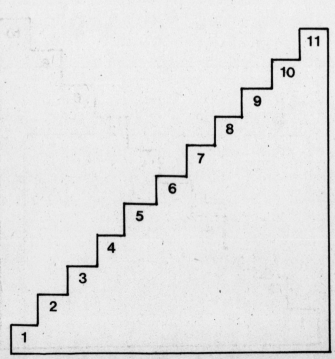

$$7 + 4 = 11$$

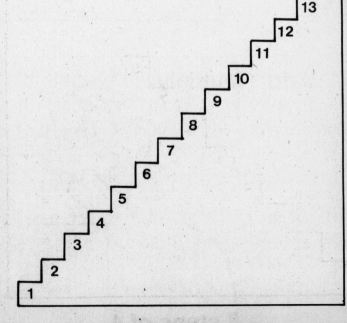

$$2 \times 7 = 14$$

Mark the steps.

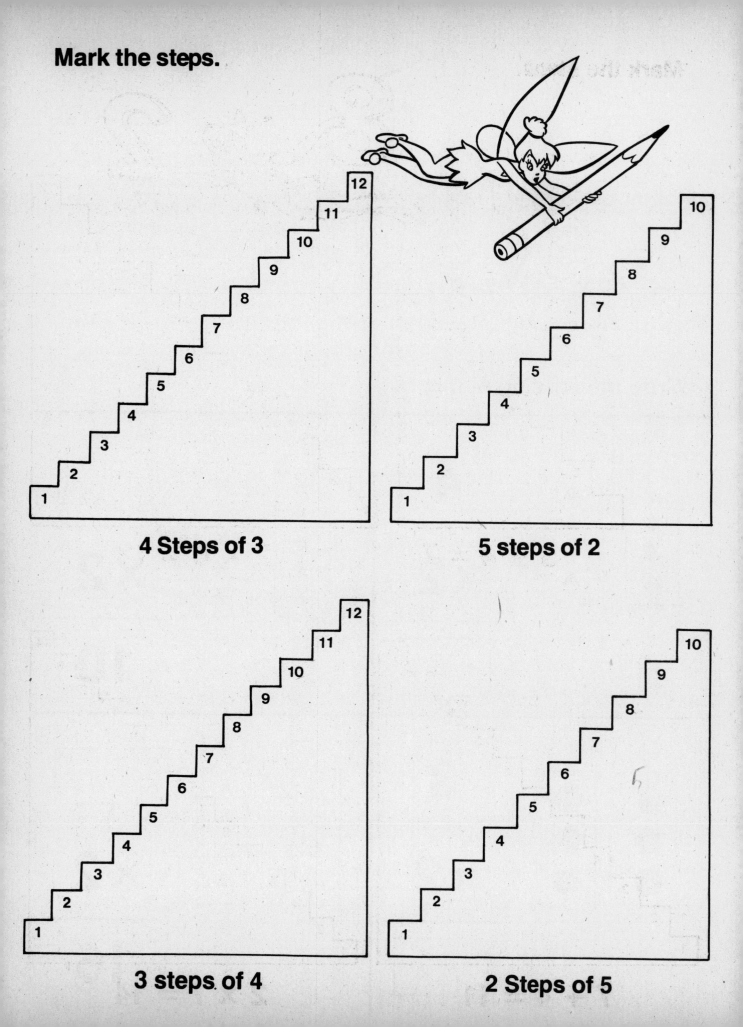

4 Steps of 3

5 steps of 2

3 steps of 4

2 Steps of 5

Write the missing numbers.

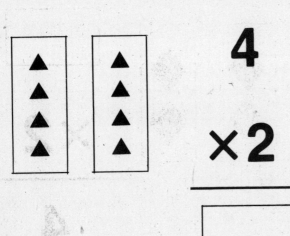

4
×2

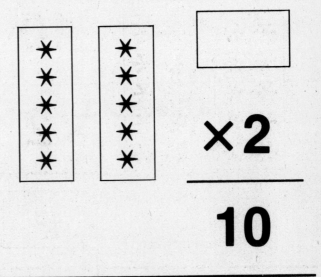

×2
10

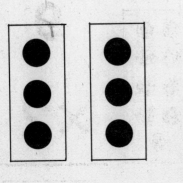

3
×2

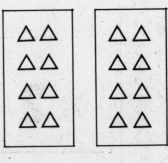

×2
16

Write the missing numbers.

$$7 \times 2 = \boxed{}$$

$$\boxed{} \times 2 = 2$$

$$10 \times 2 = \boxed{}$$

$$\boxed{} \times 2 = 4$$

$$\boxed{} \times 2 = 28$$

$$9 \times 2 = \boxed{}$$

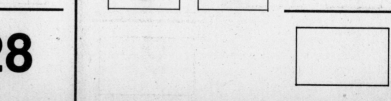

Write the missing numbers.

$$
\begin{array}{r}
2 \\
\times 3 \\
\hline \boxed{}
\end{array}
$$

$$
\begin{array}{r}
\boxed{} \\
\times 3 \\
\hline 12
\end{array}
$$

$$
\begin{array}{r}
\boxed{} \\
\times 3 \\
\hline 9
\end{array}
$$

$$
\begin{array}{r}
5 \\
\times 3 \\
\hline \boxed{}
\end{array}
$$

Write the missing numbers.

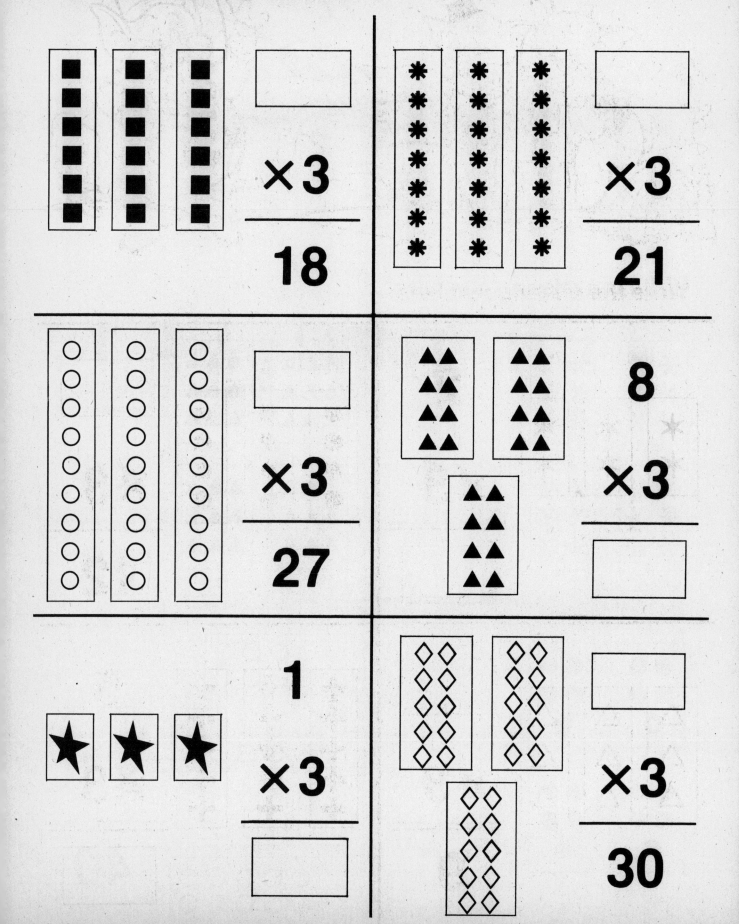

Write the missing numbers.

$$
\begin{array}{r}
6 \\
\times\,4 \\
\hline
\boxed{} \\
\end{array}
$$

$$
\begin{array}{r}
\boxed{} \\
\times\,4 \\
\hline
36 \\
\end{array}
$$

$$
\begin{array}{r}
\boxed{} \\
\times\,4 \\
\hline
20 \\
\end{array}
$$

$$
\begin{array}{r}
\boxed{} \\
\times\,4 \\
\hline
40 \\
\end{array}
$$

Write the missing numbers.

✱✱✱✱✱✱✱ ✱✱✱✱✱✱✱ ✱✱✱✱✱✱✱ ✱✱✱✱✱✱✱	7 ×4 —— ☐

💥 💥 💥 💥	☐ ×4 —— 4

■ ■ ■ ■ ■ ■ ■ ■ ■ ■ ■ ■ ■ ■	☐ ×4 —— 16

✱✱✱✱✱✱✱✱ ✱✱✱✱✱✱✱✱ ✱✱✱✱✱✱✱✱ ✱✱✱✱✱✱✱✱	8 ×4 —— ☐

❊ ❊ ❊ ❊ ❊ ❊ ❊ ❊	2 ×4 —— ☐

▶▶▶ ▶▶▶ ▶▶▶ ▶▶▶	3 ×4 —— ☐

Write the missing numbers.

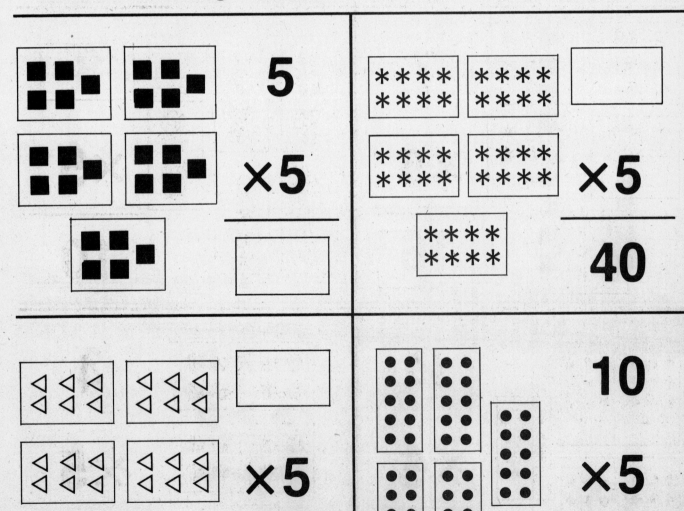

5
×5

40

30

10
×5

Write the missing numbers.

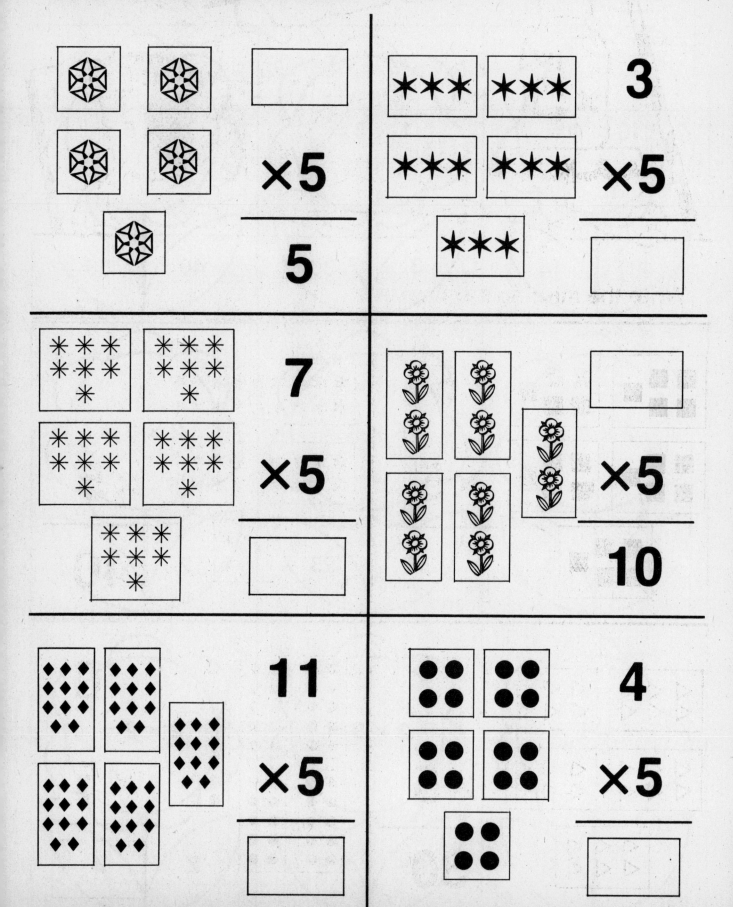

Circle each correct answer.

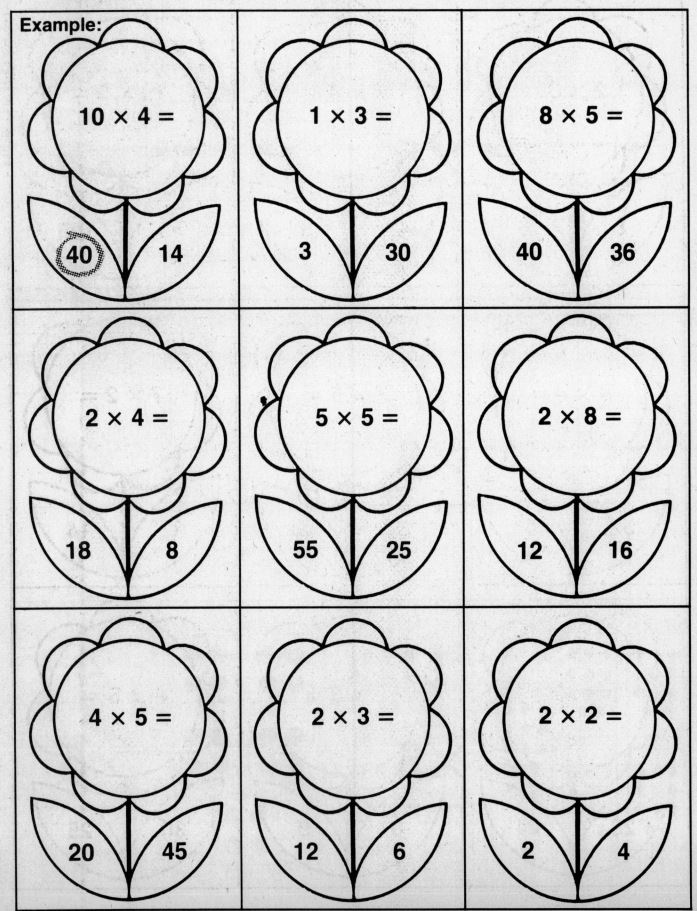

Example:

$10 \times 4 =$
40   14

$1 \times 3 =$
3   30

$8 \times 5 =$
40   36

$2 \times 4 =$
18   8

$5 \times 5 =$
55   25

$2 \times 8 =$
12   16

$4 \times 5 =$
20   45

$2 \times 3 =$
12   6

$2 \times 2 =$
2   4

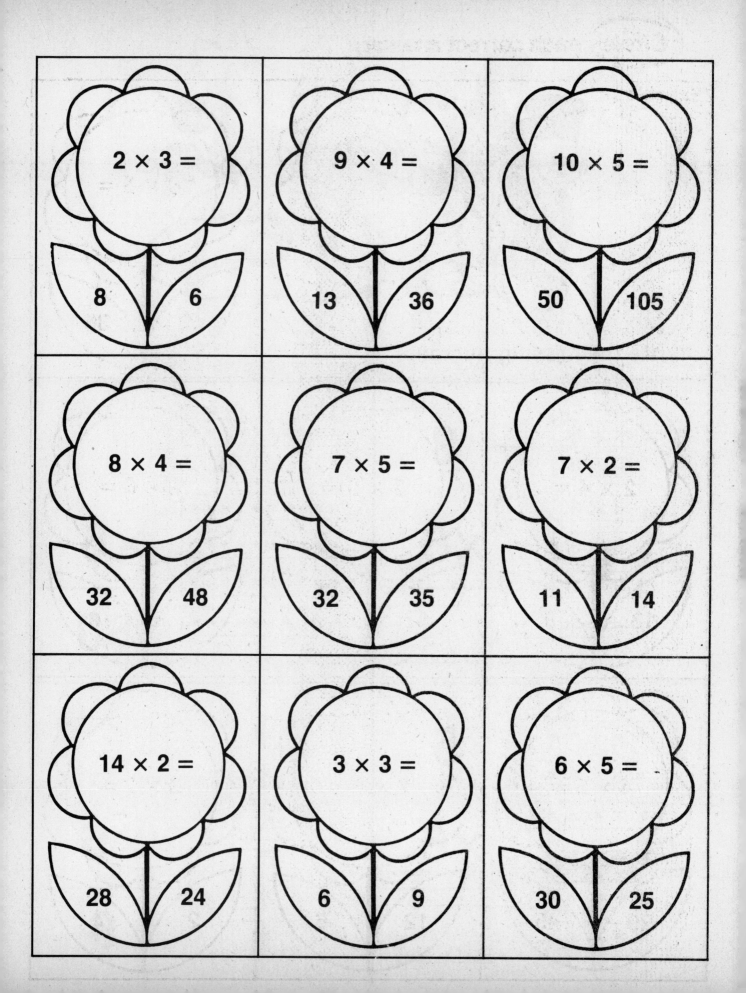

2 × 3 =   8   6

9 × 4 =   13   36

10 × 5 =   50   105

8 × 4 =   32   48

7 × 5 =   32   35

7 × 2 =   11   14

14 × 2 =   28   24

3 × 3 =   6   9

6 × 5 =   30   25

×6

Write the missing numbers.

```
***          3
***
***
***        ×6
***
***      [   ]
```

```
* * * * * * * * * *     [   ]
* * * * * * * * * *
* * * * * * * * * *
* * * * * * * * * *    ×6
* * * * * * * * * *
* * * * * * * * * *    60
```

```
* * * * *      5
* * * * *
* * * * *
* * * * *    ×6
* * * * *
* * * * *   [   ]
```

```
*          [   ]
*
*
*         ×6
*
*          6
```

Write the missing numbers.

```
* * * * * * * * *
* * * * * * * * *          9
* * * * * * * * *
* * * * * * * * *        × 6
* * * * * * * * *        _____
* * * * * * * * *         [   ]
```

```
[**] [**] [**] [**]        [    ]
[**] [**]                 × 6
                          _____
                            12
```

```
[*] [*] [*] [*] [*] [*]     8
[*] [*] [*] [*] [*] [*]
[*] [*] [*] [*] [*] [*]   × 6
[*] [*] [*] [*] [*] [*]   _____
[*] [*] [*] [*] [*] [*]     [   ]
```

```
[* * *]  [* *]           [    ]
[* * *]  [* * *]
[* * *]  [* *]          × 6
[* * *]  [* * *]        _____
[* * *]  [* * *]          66
[* * *]  [* * *]
```

```
[* * * *]                  4
[* * * *]
[* * * *]                × 6
[* * * *]                _____
[* * * *]                  [   ]
[* * * *]
```

```
[*] [*] [*] [*] [*] [*]    [    ]
[*] [*] [*] [*] [*] [*]
[*] [*] [*] [*] [*] [*]   × 6
[*] [*] [*] [*] [*] [*]   _____
[*] [*] [*] [*] [*] [*]     36
```

Write the missing numbers.

7
×7
[ ]

[ ]
×7
21

[ ]
×7
70

5
×7
[ ]

Write the missing numbers.

×7
___
63

1
×7
___

×7
___
14

8
×7
___

4
×7
___

×7
___
77

Write the missing numbers.

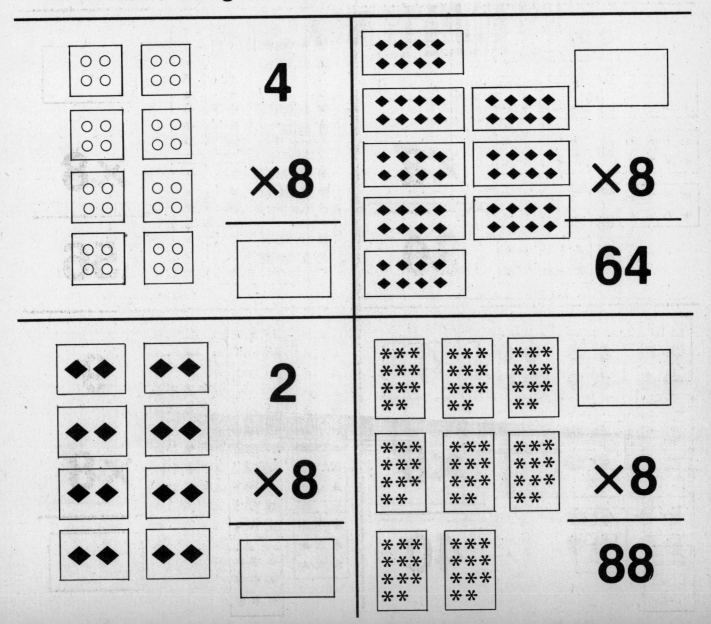

$$4 \times 8 = \boxed{}$$

$$\boxed{} \times 8 = 64$$

$$2 \times 8 = \boxed{}$$

$$\boxed{} \times 8 = 88$$

Write the missing numbers.

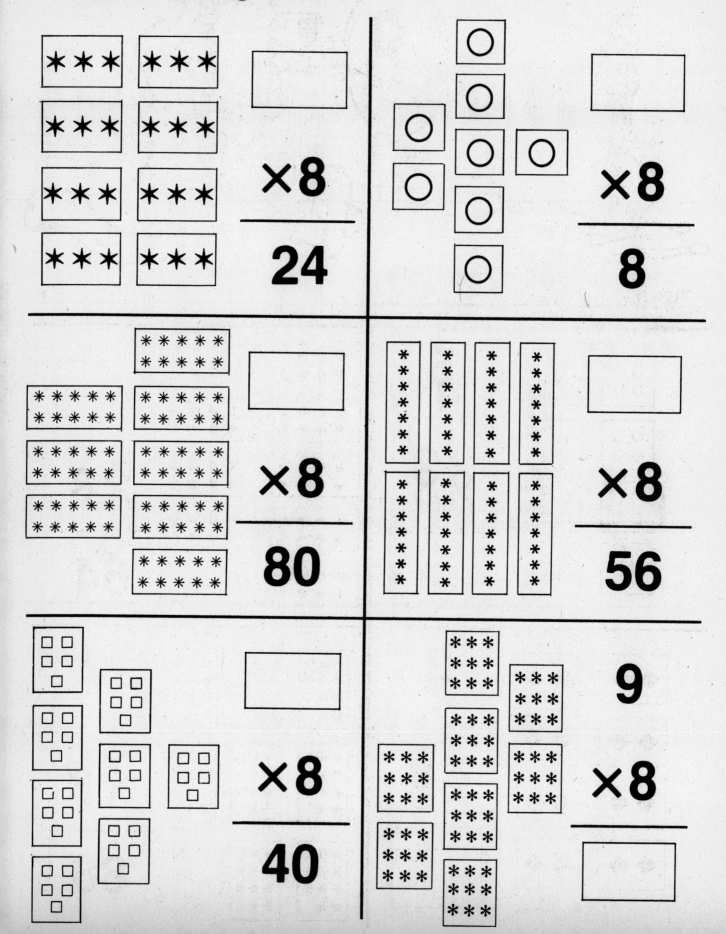

Write the missing numbers.

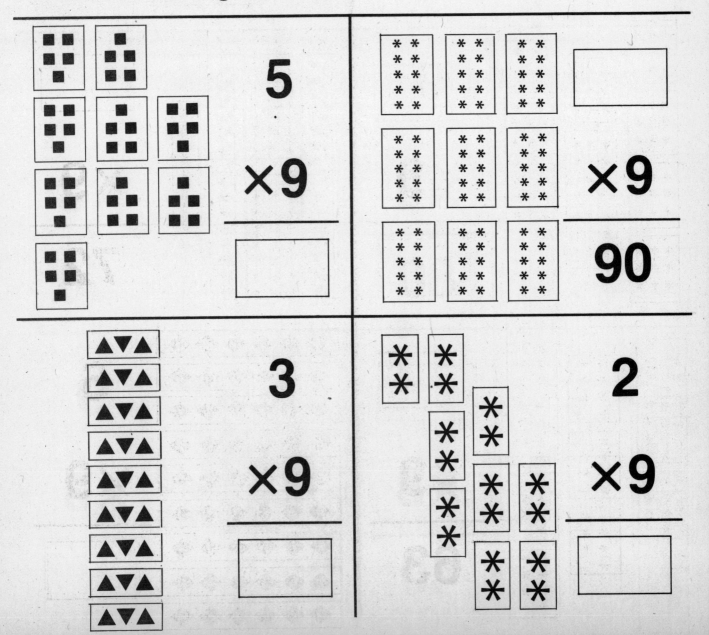

5
×9
_____

90

×9
_____
90

3
×9
_____

2
×9
_____

Write the missing numbers.

×9
___
9

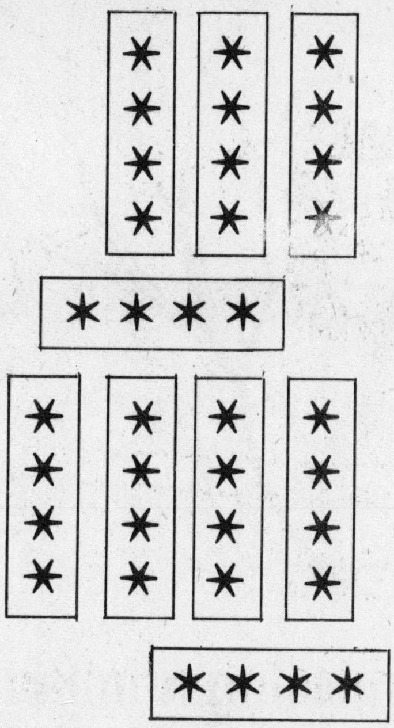

×9
___
36

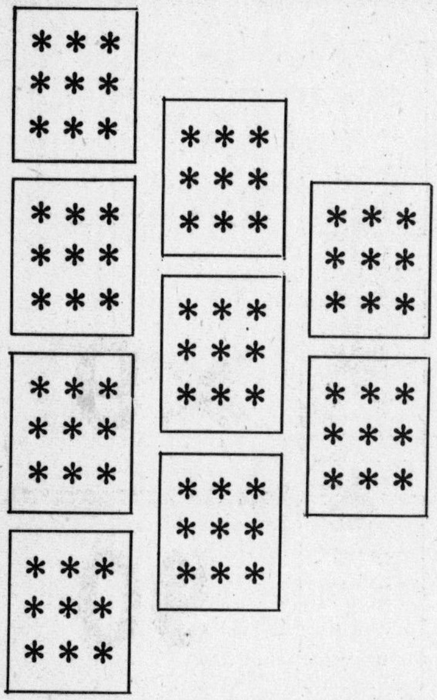

9
×9
___
[ ]

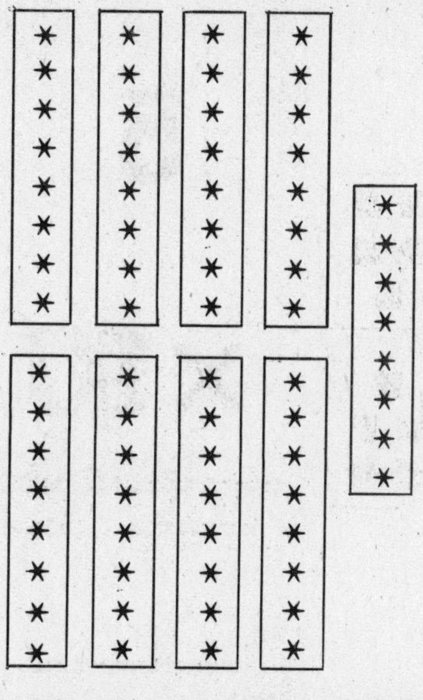

×9
___
72

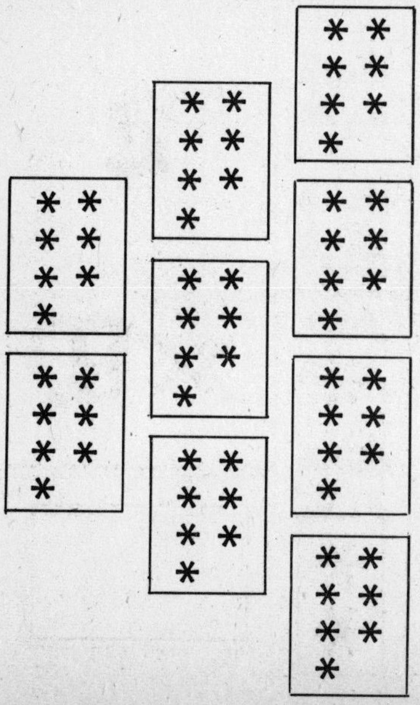

×9
___
63

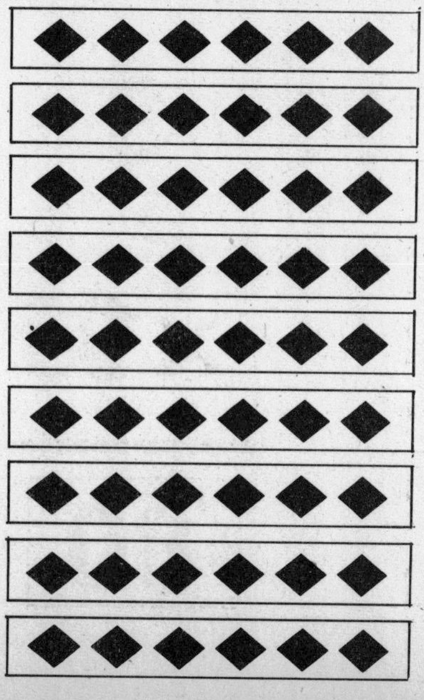

6
×9
___
[ ]

Write the missing numbers.

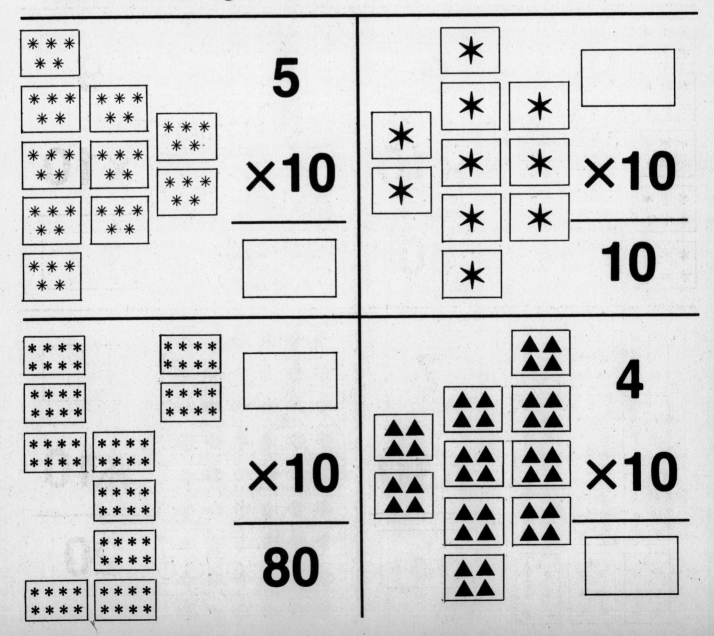

$$5 \times 10 = \boxed{}$$

$$\boxed{} \times 10 = 10$$

$$\boxed{} \times 10 = 80$$

$$4 \times 10 = \boxed{}$$

Write the missing numbers.

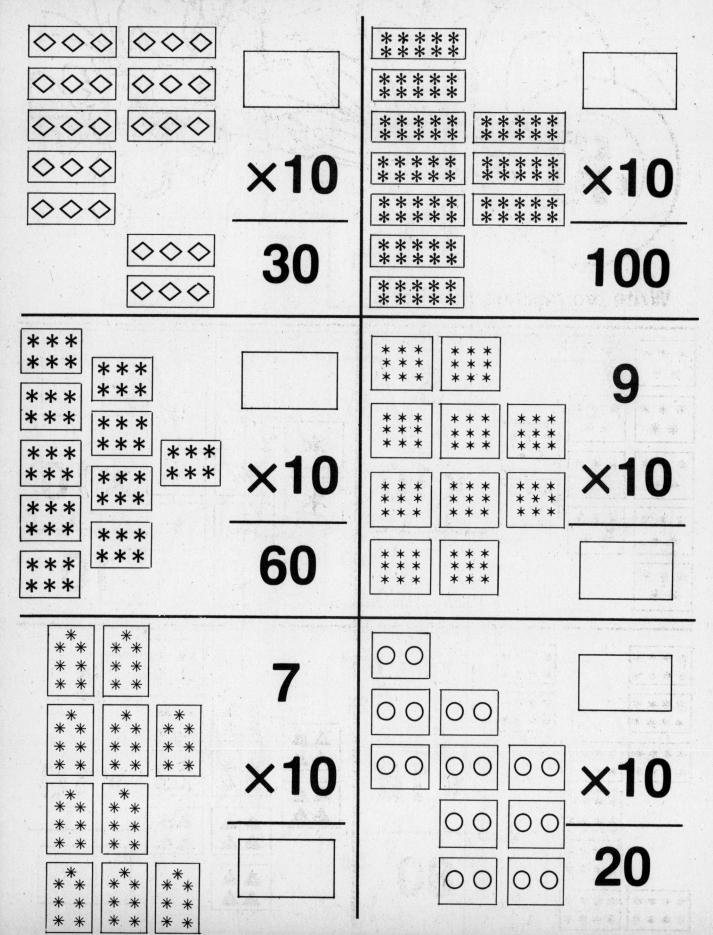

×10

30

×10

100

×10

60

9

×10

7

×10

×10

20

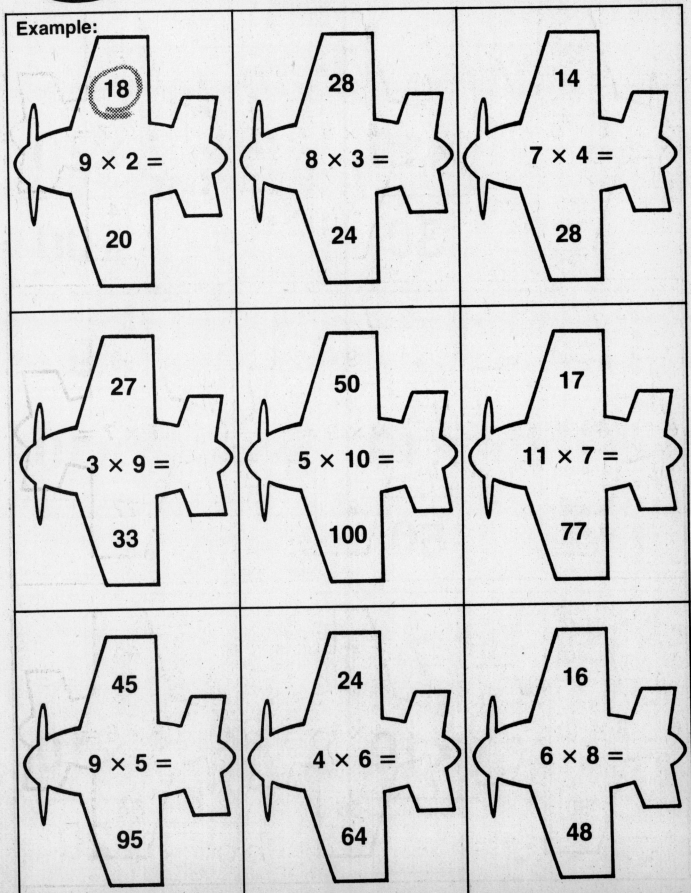

Example:

18
9 × 2 =
20

28
8 × 3 =
24

14
7 × 4 =
28

27
3 × 9 =
33

50
5 × 10 =
100

17
11 × 7 =
77

45
9 × 5 =
95

24
4 × 6 =
64

16
6 × 8 =
48

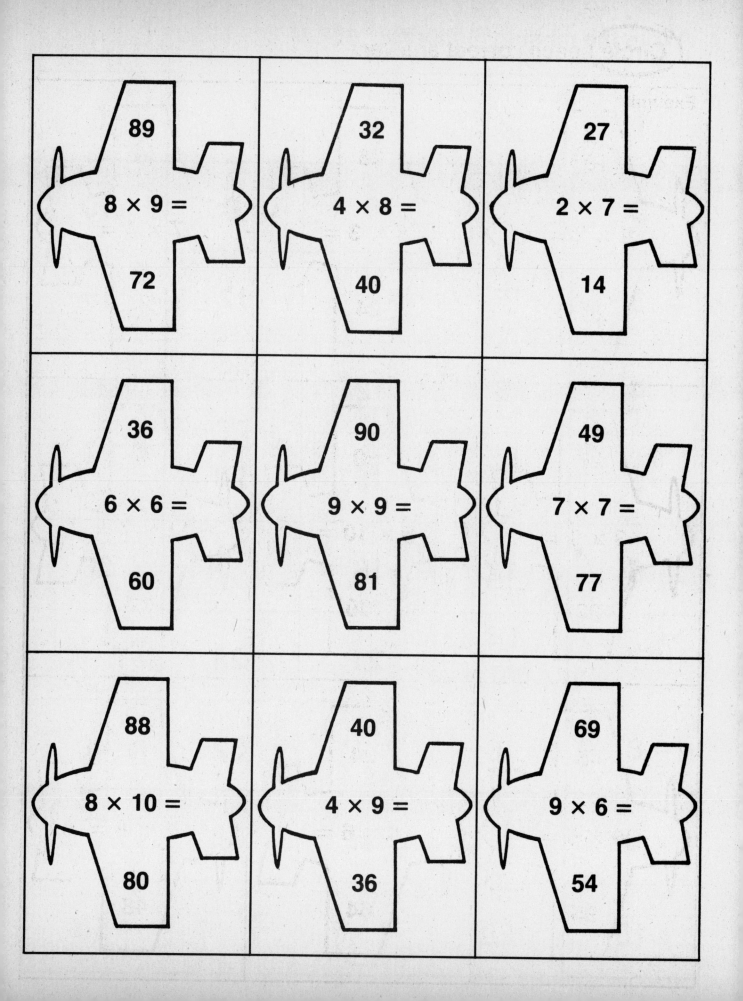

89 8 × 9 = 72	32 4 × 8 = 40	27 2 × 7 = 14
36 6 × 6 = 60	90 9 × 9 = 81	49 7 × 7 = 77
88 8 × 10 = 80	40 4 × 9 = 36	69 9 × 6 = 54

Write the missing numbers.

1	2	3	4	5
2		6	8	10
3	6		12	15
4	8	12		20
5		15	20	
6	12	18		30
7		21	28	
8	16		32	40
9		27	36	
10	20			50

6	7	8	9	10
	14	16		20
18		24	27	
	28	32		40
30	35		45	
36		48	54	
42	49		63	70
	56	64		80
54	63		81	
	70		90	

Goofy can only buy the items that have the right answer. Which ones will Goofy buy? Circle them.

Each of the Seven Dwarfs has a problem.
Help him solve it.

Doc needs 2 hats for each of the 7 Dwarfs. How many hats does he need?

Example: $2 \times 7 = 14$ _____   14 hats _____

Dopey is planting a garden. He has 5 bags, each having 10 seeds. How many seeds does he have?

_____ _____ seeds

Grumpy is building a fence. Each part has four boards in it. To build 5 parts, how many boards will he need?

_____ _____ boards

Happy is planting trees in the forest. He plants 6 trees in each of 3 rows. How many trees will he plant in all?

_____ _____ trees

Sleepy counts sheep when he sleeps. If he sees 5 sheep every minute for 5 minutes, how many sheep does he see altogether?

_____ _____ sheep

Bashful changes tires on 4-wheel trucks. If he puts new sets of tires on 8 trucks, how many tires will he have changed?

_____ _____ tires

Sneezy uses 3 handkerchiefs a day, every day. How many handkerchiefs does he use in a week?

_____ _____ handkerchiefs

Uncle Scrooge has to set up 36 boxes in the window of his grocery store. He can stack them in different ways. Draw the boxes in each window below.

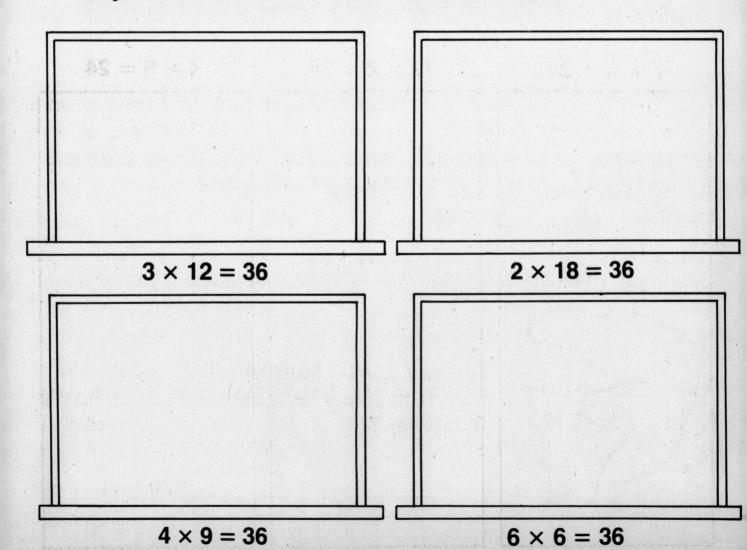

$3 \times 12 = 36$

$2 \times 18 = 36$

$4 \times 9 = 36$

$6 \times 6 = 36$

Pluto has a booth at the fair. To win a game, a player must knock over all 24 pins with one ball. In the spaces below, draw 3 ways Pluto can set up his pins.

$8 \times 3 = 24$	$12 \times 2 = 24$	$4 \times 6 = 24$

Write the number of plants in each part of Winnie the Pooh's garden.

Example: 2 × 4 = 8

_____

_____

_____

Draw a line from each bird to the correct number.

4×4

6×2

48

2×10

20

8×6

36

1×8

2×8

4×3

12×4

The 101 Dalmatians have escaped. Find out where the dogs belong. Draw a line from each dog to the correct number home.

Help Donald teach his nephews how to multiply. Correct each one's homework. Fill in the correct answers.

HUEY

8	4	9
×7	×7	×7
58	28	64

4	6	5
×8	×8	×8
33	48	30

3	5	8
×9	×9	×9
27	46	71

DEWEY

10	10	10
×3	×8	×4
30	88	40

6	6	6
×5	×9	×7
31	55	43

2	2	2
×8	×5	×2
17	9	4

LOUIE

2	4	8
×5	×5	×5
7	21	45

3	5	6
×3	×3	×3
9	15	66

1	8	7
×4	×4	×4
4	33	28

Help the ringmaster set up for the circus.
Solve his problems.

While the circus is in town each elephant eats 1 bag of food 3 times a day. If the circus is in town for 5 days, how many bags of food will each elephant eat?

Example: $3 \times 5 = 15$ 15 **bags**

The clowns use 5 make-up sticks each day. How many will they use in 5 days?

_____ _____ **sticks**

The ticket seller sells 10 tickets per hour. How many will he sell in 5 hours?

_____ _____ **tickets**

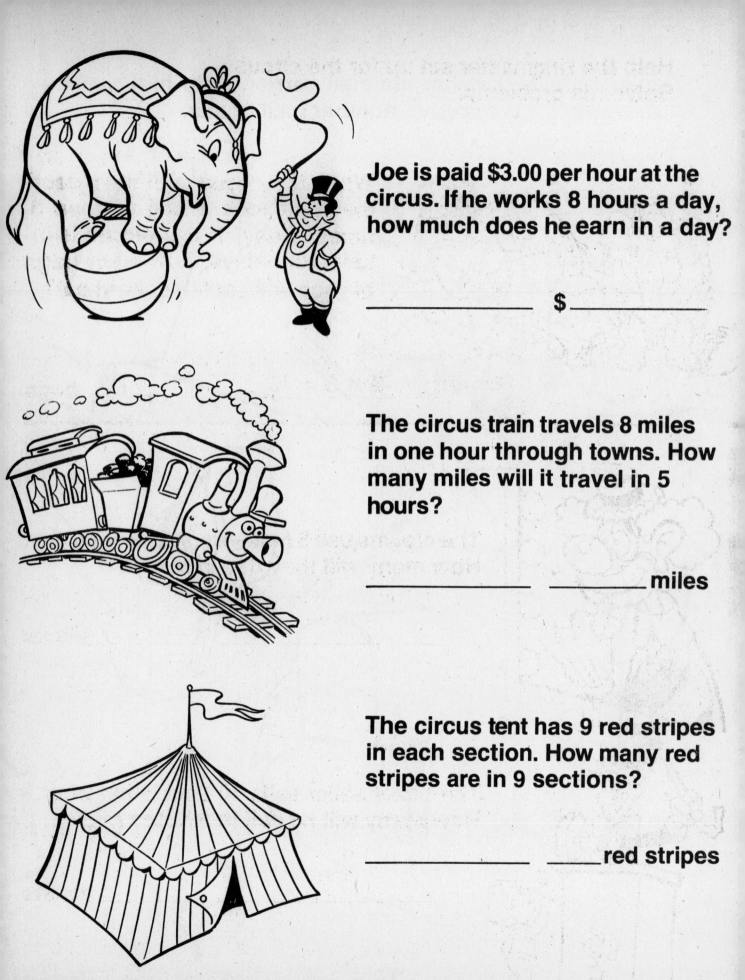

Joe is paid $3.00 per hour at the circus. If he works 8 hours a day, how much does he earn in a day?

_____ $ _____

The circus train travels 8 miles in one hour through towns. How many miles will it travel in 5 hours?

_____ _____ miles

The circus tent has 9 red stripes in each section. How many red stripes are in 9 sections?

_____ _____ red stripes

Donald Duck is helping the mail carrier. Help him put the mail in the correct number mail boxes.

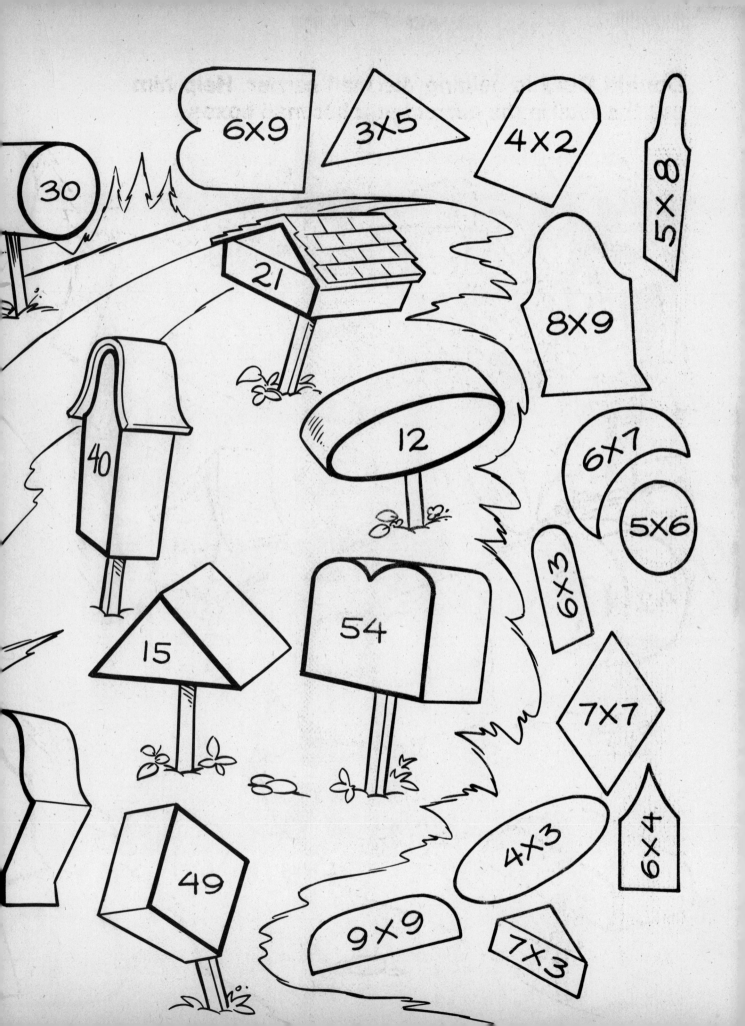

Put the players at the correct number bases.

The <u>ones</u> wheel.
Write the numbers. Color the wheel.

The <u>twos</u> wheel.

Write the numbers. Color the wheel.

The <u>threes</u> wheel.

Write the numbers. Color the wheel.

The <u>fours</u> wheel.

Write the numbers. Color the wheel.

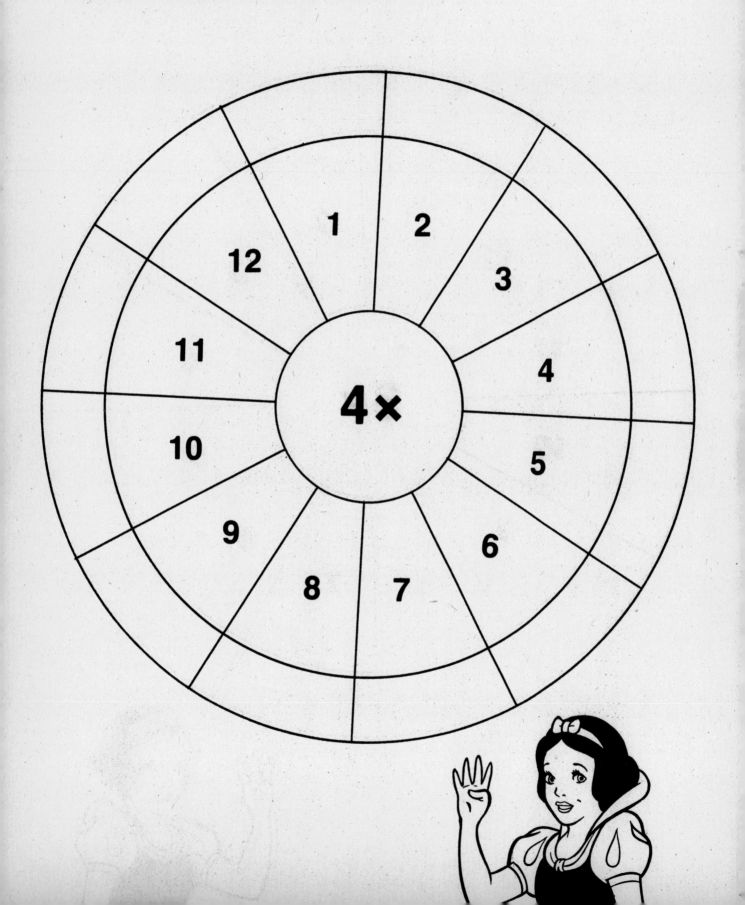

The <u>fives</u> wheel.

Write the numbers. Color the wheel.

1 2 3 4 5 6 7 8 9 10 11 12

5×

The <u>sixes</u> wheel.

Write the numbers. Color the wheel.

The sevens wheel.

Write the numbers. Color the wheel.

The eights wheel.

Write the numbers. Color the wheel.

The <u>nines</u> wheel.

Write the numbers. Color the wheel.

The <u>tens</u> wheel.

Write the numbers. Color the wheel.

Match the numbers.

$3 \times 18 =$

$4 \times 12 =$

$3 \times 24 =$

$4 \times 3 =$

$3 \times 16 =$

$2 \times 36 =$

$5 \times 10 =$

$8 \times 6 =$

$2 \times 6 =$

$6 \times 12 =$

$2 \times 25 =$

$6 \times 9 =$

$9 \times 8 =$

$2 \times 27 =$

Make your own Pinocchio puppet.
Cut out the pieces. Match the answers to the
problems by pasting the pieces on Pinocchio.
Color him.